Guest name

Comments

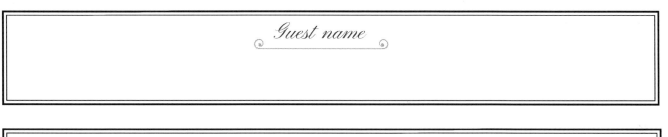

Guest name

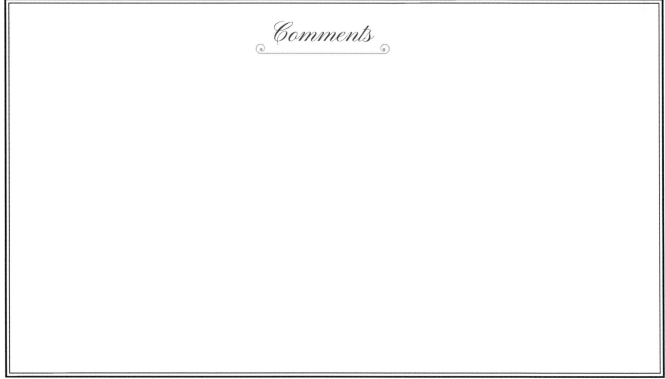

Comments

Guest name

Comments

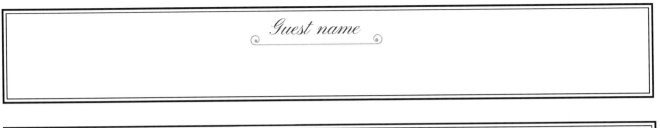

Guest name

Comments

Guest name

Comments

Guest name

Comments

Guest name

Comments

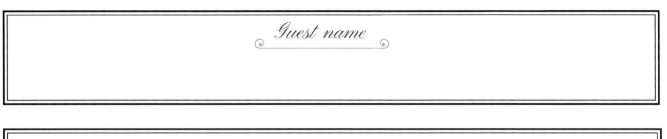

Guest name

Comments

Guest name

Comments

Guest name

Comments

Guest name

Comments

Guest name

Comments

Guest name

Comments

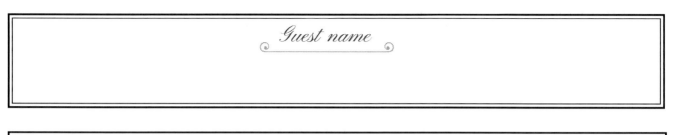

Guest name

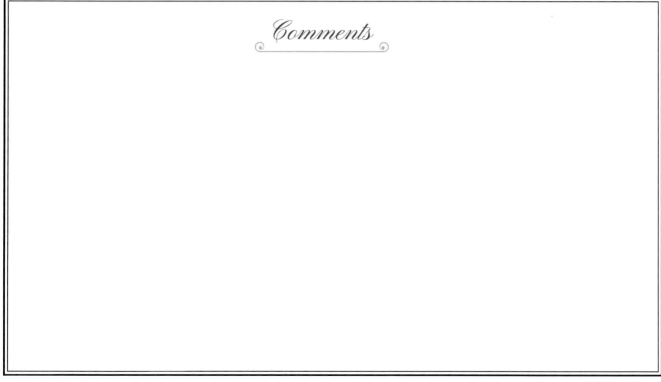

Comments

Guest name

Comments

Guest name

Comments

Guest name

Comments

Guest name

Comments

Guest name

Comments

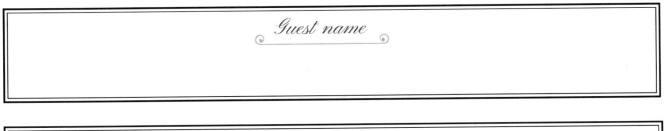

Guest name

Comments

Guest name

Comments

Guest name

Comments

Guest name

Comments

Guest name

Comments

Guest name

Comments

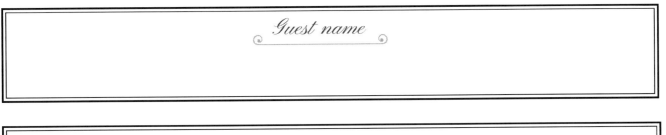

Guest name

Comments

Guest name

Comments

Guest name

Comments

Guest name

Comments

Guest name

Comments

Guest name

Comments

Guest name

Comments

Guest name

Comments

Guest name

Comments

Guest name

Comments

Guest name

Comments

Guest name

Comments

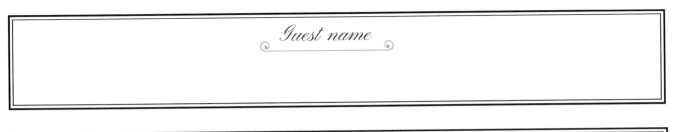

Guest name

Comments

Guest name

Comments

Guest name

Comments

Guest name

Comments

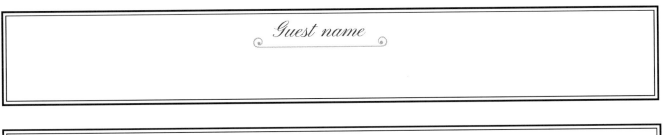

Guest name

Comments

Guest name

Comments

Guest name

Comments

Guest name

Comments

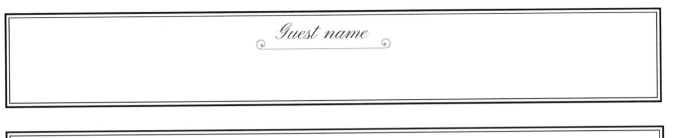

Guest name

Comments

Guest name

Comments

Guest name

Comments

Guest name

Comments

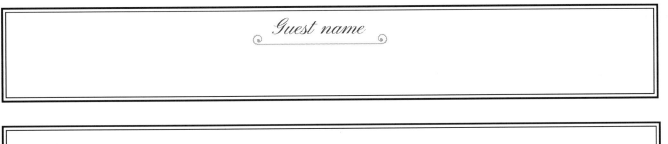

Guest name

Comments

Guest name

Comments

Guest name

Comments

Guest name

Comments

Guest name

Comments

Guest name

Comments

Guest name

Comments

Guest name

Comments

Guest name

Comments

Guest name

Comments

Guest name

Comments

Guest name

Comments

Guest name

Comments

Guest name

Comments

Guest name

Comments

Guest name

Comments

Guest name

Comments

Guest name

Comments

Guest name

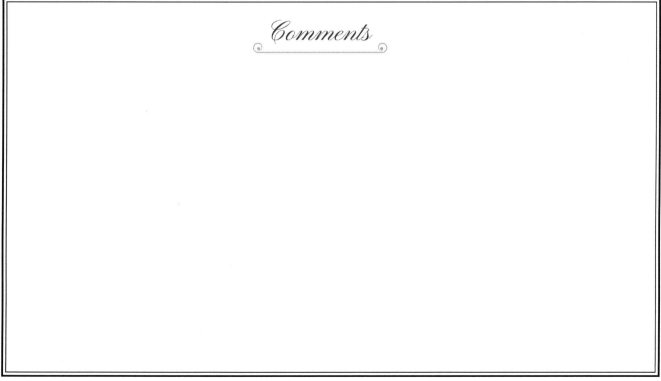

Comments

Guest name

Comments

Guest name

Comments

Guest name

Comments

Guest name

Comments

Guest name

Comments

Guest name

Comments

Guest name

Comments

Guest name

Comments

Guest name

Comments

Guest name

Comments

Guest name

Comments

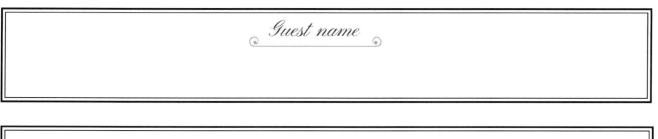

Guest name

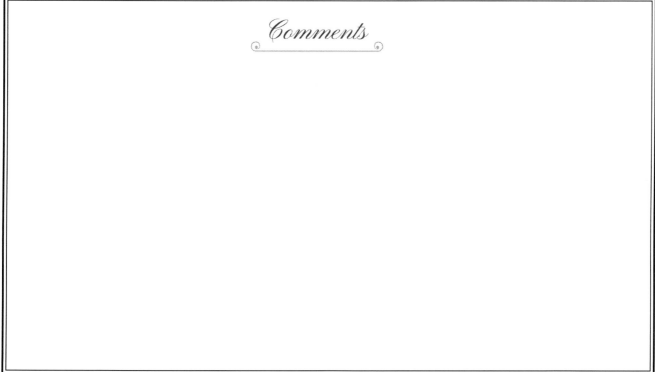

Comments

Guest name

Comments

Guest name

Comments

Guest name

Comments

Guest name

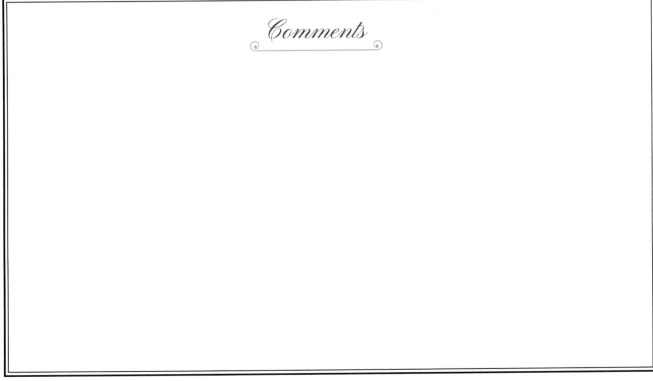

Comments

Guest name

Comments

Guest name

Comments

Guest name

Comments

Guest name

Comments

Guest name

Comments

Guest name

Comments

Guest name

Comments

Guest name

Comments

Guest name

Comments

Guest name

Comments

Guest name

Comments

Guest name

Comments

Guest name

Comments

Guest name

Comments

Guest name

Comments

Guest name

Comments

Made in the USA
Columbia, SC
12 July 2022

63371072R00057